THIS IS YOUR

~~GOOD BAD~~

REAL LIFE

TIME TO

FOCUS ON WHAT MATTERS
& LIVE IT EVERY DAY.

Name: _____   Start Date: /   /

GET REAL:

*What do you hope God does in and through your life
as you center in Him over the next 30 days?*

FREE STARTER KIT

Don't do one more thing until you go to **charityreeb.com** and sign up for your **FREE Starter Kit.**

The kit includes:

- **Method-at-a-glance video and PDF** - In 5 minutes or less, learn how to maximize this journal.

- **The Life List** - Make the most of each week with this comprehensive life checklist that streamlines all of life's priorities.

- **Motivation** - Get weekly emails and texts to help you stay on track.

- **Community** - Gain access to the live virtual hangout and the private Facebook community.

Hi, I'm Charity!

I created this journal because I needed it.

My life from the outside looked like I had it all together.

I had worked with ministries and nonprofits in more than 60 countries, started numerous successful movements and businesses, and received accolades for all of it. It was work for God and the good of the world.

But I remember thinking when I would receive praise from people, *Don't look too closely.* My life from the inside was a mess.

Turns out working for God is not an adequate replacement for relationship with God. Granted, I tried. I downloaded and bought every app, devotional, and self-help book on the market. I would set resolutions to start journaling. Inevitably, it never took long for me to feel overwhelmed and quit.

. . . .

Truth is, I had been a believer in Jesus my entire life, and I still struggled with basic spiritual essentials like prayer, reading the Word, meditation, and sharing my faith regularly with others.

. . . .

When my third child, Samara, was born, I was forced to slow down. This slowing allowed me the opportunity to face the truth: I was doing good, but I was not savoring the good God had for me.

I remember looking into Samara's eyes when she was born and thinking, *I want you and your brothers to have a mother whose life is prioritized in the right order: God, family, friends, my own health, then work.*

When I got home from the hospital, I began to think about my need to re-center my life in the Spirit. I wanted to put together an action plan to align my priorities with my real life.

I'll never forget the morning I searched online for a journal to help guide me. Over and over again I searched, "Spirit-centered life journal" in different forms. Most of the journals and planners I found focused on life achievements, but what about the things I held most dear? That was when the idea for *The Real Life Journal* was sparked.

· ·

It's a journal unlike any other, a guide that de-compartmentalizes real life and spirituality.

· ·

I CREATED THIS JOURNAL TO HELP ME DO FOUR THINGS

1   *Activate my priorities*
by giving me a framework for evaluating what I need to focus on in any given week.

2   *Center in the Spirit*
daily through prayer, Bible comprehension, and scripture meditation.

3   *Never forget life's moments*
because I'm journaling daily within a simple and efficient framework.

4   *Share life*
by engaging in community and accountability.

I can honestly say even after creating and using this method, my life is still crazy-busy. But, my faith in Jesus is stronger, I have more joy than I've ever had, I'm healthier than I have ever been both physically and spiritually, and this planner acts as a seamless guide as I wade through life's clutter with Jesus.

I trust as you make an intentional effort to be real with God in the next 30 days, it is going to be a transformational experience.

Best,

Charity

HERE'S HOW IT WORKS

AN OVERVIEW OF THE WEEKS AHEAD

DAY 1

LIFE INVENTORY – *30 minutes*

- Use the Life Circle to center in the Spirit and identify your priorities.

  - Set 3 focus goals.

  - Calendarize them.

  - Live for what matters most to you!

DAYS 2-7

SPIRITUAL ESSENTIALS & JOURNALING – *10 minutes each day*

- Practice spiritual essentials.

- Remember life's moments.

- Bring your focus goals to life.

- Celebrate progress with your week-in-review.

EACH WEEK

SHARE LIFE – *As little or as much time as you want.*

- Be accountable and practice spiritual essentials with friends you trust.

- Get real about goals and progress.

- Encourage each other.

BEFORE YOU START

INVITE SOMEONE TO DO THIS WITH YOU.

Make it easy on yourself to be accountable—instead of seeking new friends to be accountable to, weave accountability into the fabric of your current life.

You could partner up with your workout buddy, a small group you're already a part of, your church, a close friend you see regularly, or, if you're married, your spouse.

WHO: _____

WHEN: _____

WHERE: _____

SET A WEEKLY 30-MINUTE DATE WITH YOURSELF FOR LIFE INVENTORY.

If you're wondering where you're going to fit this into your already-crazy schedule, keep in mind it's worth it.

In my own calculations, I save an average of 8 hours a week when it is planned out according to this method.

Your first inventory may take you a bit longer than it will in the future. It gets easier.

Plan ahead by putting all of your inventory times on your calendar. Think ahead about obstacles.

WHEN: _____

WHERE: _____

DON'T FORGET

I'M HERE TO HELP.

Download your Starter Kit at **charityreeb.com** for method-at-a-glance videos and PDF tutorials. You'll get explanations and tips to help you establish the practical disciplines found within this journal.

LET'S GET STARTED!

Start by taking a moment to express your belief in Jesus to Him. Acknowledge that the power to change your life lies in your willingness to recognize where true strength comes from. Alone, without God, you will never fully succeed. If you find yourself not believing, that's ok. Be honest about that. Express it to God and ask for help. Read Mark 9:23–24. This man's son needed healing. Jesus asked him if he believed, and the man was honest, *"I believe, but help me in my unbelief!"* Jesus saw his sincerity and healed his son, leaving him firmly believing for a lifetime.

LIVE FOR WHAT MATTERS • DIE WITHOUT REGRET

Focus
your life
on what
matters
most
to you.

THE LIFE CIRCLE

The Life Circle is a quick guide for you to evaluate your holistic health, adapted from Paul J. Meyer's Wheel of Life.

Your spirit is in the center of the circle to help you remember to evaluate each segment from an eternal perspective. Each area of the circle represents an aspect of life about which you will ask yourself, "Do I feel satisfied or unsatisfied?" Then, color in the slice accordingly.

Life Circle – Example

3 TIPS FOR THE LIFE CIRCLE EXERCISE.

1

Perfect balance may not be realistic.

The goal of this exercise is to bring awareness and healing to areas of life that may need focus. You may never have a week when your Life Circle is in perfect balance. That is ok.

2

Be nice to yourself.

If there is an area of your life that is severely or chronically out of balance, don't get down on yourself. Simply acknowledge it and draw your awareness to it as you set your goals for the week. Tell your group and ask for support.

3

Life happens.

There are seasons in life that you may need to give yourself permission to be out of balance to reach a goal, or you may have circumstances that are out of your control that are throwing you out of balance. That's real life. Commit those things to God daily and ask Him to show you how to be spiritually healthy in spite of circumstances.

CHECK IN WITH YOURSELF

✸ LIFE CIRCLE | *5 minutes*

Use the Life Circle as a tool to ask yourself, "Do I feel satisfied or unsatisfied?" in each area. Fill in each slice accordingly.

⊕ ASK YOURSELF WHY | *5 minutes*

Why are some slices fuller and others emptier? Talk to God and ask for wisdom.

🏆 SET FOCUS GOALS | *10 minutes*

Set 1 goal for 3 areas of the Life Circle you would like to focus on this week. Keep all goals specific and measurable, **then write down how you are going to prioritize it into your week.**

LIFE CIRCLE FOCUS AREA & GOAL	PRIORITIZE IT

☑ **LIFE LIST** | **OPTIONAL** | *10 minutes*

Do you need a comprehensive checklist to guide you through each category of the Life Circle?

It's called the Life List and it's FREE at **charityreeb.com**.

Consider using the Life List on weeks when you're feeling overwhelmed or need help making each area of the Life Circle actionable.

⊞ BLOCK YOUR SCHEDULE | *10 minutes*

Your schedule reflects your priorities. Write in your 3 focus goals for this week, then build the rest of your schedule around them. Use a pencil so you can erase and rearrange.

	MORNING	AFTERNOON	NIGHT
M			
T			
W			
T			
F			
S			
S			

⚖️ BALANCE THE YESES AND NOES | *10 minutes*

Ask yourself, "What am I saying no to by saying yes to everything on this schedule? Will I regret that no?"

📦 UNPACK IT | *5 minutes*

Are you overcommitted? Intentionally lighten your load by either deferring something to next week or, when possible, asking someone for help.

Spiritual disciplines produce real results in every area of life.

SPIRITUAL ESSENTIALS

day one

READ anything from the Bible. Jot down what you read.

LEARN AND APPLY it to your real life. Jot down what you learned.

COMMIT concerns to God.

CONVERSE with God. Write a synopsis of your conversation.

MEDITATE on a word, theme, or verse found in scripture. Keep it true, pure, and positive.

JOURNALING

DEBRIEF the day.

A MOMENT you don't want to forget.

3 FOCUS GOALS Fill in or check boxes as you complete.

THOUGHTS and scribbles.

2

SPIRITUAL ESSENTIALS

READ anything from the Bible. Jot down what you read.

LEARN AND APPLY it to your real life. Jot down what you learned.

COMMIT concerns to God.

CONVERSE with God. Write a synopsis of your conversation.

MEDITATE on a word, theme, or verse found in scripture. Keep it true, pure, and positive.

JOURNALING

DEBRIEF the day.

A MOMENT you don't want to forget.

3 FOCUS GOALS Fill in or check boxes as you complete.

THOUGHTS and scribbles.

SPIRITUAL ESSENTIALS

READ anything from the Bible. Jot down what you read.

LEARN AND APPLY it to your real life. Jot down what you learned.

COMMIT concerns to God.

CONVERSE with God. Write a synopsis of your conversation.

MEDITATE on a word, theme, or verse found in scripture. Keep it true, pure, and positive.

JOURNALING

DEBRIEF the day.

A MOMENT you don't want to forget.

3 FOCUS GOALS Fill in or check boxes as you complete.

THOUGHTS and scribbles.

SPIRITUAL ESSENTIALS

4

READ anything from the Bible. Jot down what you read.

LEARN AND APPLY it to your real life. Jot down what you learned.

COMMIT concerns to God.

CONVERSE with God. Write a synopsis of your conversation.

MEDITATE on a word, theme, or verse found in scripture. Keep it true, pure, and positive.

JOURNALING

DEBRIEF the day.

A MOMENT you don't want to forget.

3 FOCUS GOALS Fill in or check boxes as you complete.

THOUGHTS and scribbles.

SPIRITUAL ESSENTIALS

READ anything from the Bible. Jot down what you read.

LEARN AND APPLY it to your real life. Jot down what you learned.

COMMIT concerns to God.

CONVERSE with God. Write a synopsis of your conversation.

MEDITATE on a word, theme, or verse found in scripture. Keep it true, pure, and positive.

JOURNALING

DEBRIEF the day.

A MOMENT you don't want to forget.

3 FOCUS GOALS Fill in or check boxes as you complete.

THOUGHTS and scribbles.

SPIRITUAL ESSENTIALS

READ anything from the Bible. Jot down what you read.

LEARN AND APPLY it to your real life. Jot down what you learned.

COMMIT concerns to God.

CONVERSE with God. Write a synopsis of your conversation.

MEDITATE on a word, theme, or verse found in scripture. Keep it true, pure, and positive.

JOURNALING

DEBRIEF the day.

A MOMENT you don't want to forget.

3 FOCUS GOALS Fill in or check boxes as you complete.

THOUGHTS and scribbles.

WEEK-IN-REVIEW

Revisit your 3 focus goals and write down how you've done.

What were the highlights of the week? Victories? Defeats?

What did you learn about God this week?

What did you learn about yourself this week?

SHARE LIFE

TALK ABOUT

- Your conversations with God this week
- What you are learning and applying to your life from the Bible
- Whom you are investing in who doesn't know Jesus
- Any movement toward or away from your 3 focus goals

CONVERSATION NOTES:

What have you learned from each other?

How will you support and encourage each other this week? *Put a reminder on your calendar so you don't forget.*

NOTES or thoughts from the week.

LIVE FOR WHAT MATTERS · DIE WITHOUT REGRET

You have everything you need in Jesus to live life to the fullest.

CHECK IN WITH YOURSELF

✳ **LIFE CIRCLE** | *5 minutes*

Use the Life Circle as a tool to ask yourself, "Do I feel satisfied or unsatisfied?" in each area. Fill in each slice accordingly.

⊕ **ASK YOURSELF WHY** | *5 minutes*

Why are some slices fuller and others emptier? Talk to God and ask for wisdom.

🏆 SET FOCUS GOALS | *10 minutes*

Set 1 goal for 3 areas of the Life Circle you would like to focus on this week. Keep all goals specific and measurable, **then write down how you are going to prioritize it into your week.**

LIFE CIRCLE FOCUS AREA & GOAL	PRIORITIZE IT

☑ LIFE LIST | OPTIONAL | *10 minutes*

Do you need a comprehensive checklist to guide you through each category of the Life Circle?

It's called the Life List and it's FREE at **charityreeb.com**.

Consider using the Life List on weeks when you're feeling overwhelmed or need help making each area of the Life Circle actionable.

(Photo of the downloadable list maker)

🗓 **BLOCK YOUR SCHEDULE** | *10 minutes*

Your schedule reflects your priorities. Write in your 3 focus goals for this week, then build the rest of your schedule around them. Use a pencil so you can erase and rearrange.

	MORNING	AFTERNOON	NIGHT
M			
T			
W			
T			
F			
S			
S			

⚖ BALANCE THE YESES AND NOES | *10 minutes*

Ask yourself, "What am I saying no to by saying yes to everything on this schedule? Will I regret that no?"

📦 UNPACK IT | *5 minutes*

Are you overcommitted? Intentionally lighten your load by either deferring something to next week or, when possible, asking someone for help.

Allow God
to do
what
you cannot
do alone.

SPIRITUAL ESSENTIALS

READ anything from the Bible. Jot down what you read.

LEARN AND APPLY it to your real life. Jot down what you learned.

COMMIT concerns to God.

CONVERSE with God. Write a synopsis of your conversation.

MEDITATE on a word, theme, or verse found in scripture. Keep it true, pure, and positive.

1

JOURNALING

DEBRIEF the day.

A MOMENT you don't want to forget.

3 FOCUS GOALS Fill in or check boxes as you complete.

☐ _____   ☐ _____   ☐ _____

THOUGHTS and scribbles.

SPIRITUAL ESSENTIALS

READ anything from the Bible. Jot down what you read.

LEARN AND APPLY it to your real life. Jot down what you learned.

COMMIT concerns to God.

CONVERSE with God. Write a synopsis of your conversation.

MEDITATE on a word, theme, or verse found in scripture. Keep it true, pure, and positive.

2

JOURNALING

DEBRIEF the day.

A MOMENT you don't want to forget.

3 FOCUS GOALS Fill in or check boxes as you complete.

THOUGHTS and scribbles.

SPIRITUAL ESSENTIALS

READ anything from the Bible. Jot down what you read.

LEARN AND APPLY it to your real life. Jot down what you learned.

COMMIT concerns to God.

CONVERSE with God. Write a synopsis of your conversation.

MEDITATE on a word, theme, or verse found in scripture. Keep it true, pure, and positive.

JOURNALING

DEBRIEF the day.

A MOMENT you don't want to forget.

3 FOCUS GOALS Fill in or check boxes as you complete.

THOUGHTS and scribbles.

SPIRITUAL ESSENTIALS

4

READ anything from the Bible. Jot down what you read.

LEARN AND APPLY it to your real life. Jot down what you learned.

COMMIT concerns to God.

CONVERSE with God. Write a synopsis of your conversation.

MEDITATE on a word, theme, or verse found in scripture. Keep it true, pure, and positive.

JOURNALING

DEBRIEF the day.

A MOMENT you don't want to forget.

3 FOCUS GOALS Fill in or check boxes as you complete.

THOUGHTS and scribbles.

SPIRITUAL ESSENTIALS

READ anything from the Bible. Jot down what you read.

LEARN AND APPLY it to your real life. Jot down what you learned.

COMMIT concerns to God.

CONVERSE with God. Write a synopsis of your conversation.

MEDITATE on a word, theme, or verse found in scripture. Keep it true, pure, and positive.

5

JOURNALING

DEBRIEF the day.

A MOMENT you don't want to forget.

3 FOCUS GOALS Fill in or check boxes as you complete.

THOUGHTS and scribbles.

SPIRITUAL ESSENTIALS

READ anything from the Bible. Jot down what you read.

LEARN AND APPLY it to your real life. Jot down what you learned.

COMMIT concerns to God.

CONVERSE with God. Write a synopsis of your conversation.

MEDITATE on a word, theme, or verse found in scripture. Keep it true, pure, and positive.

JOURNALING

DEBRIEF the day.

A MOMENT you don't want to forget.

3 FOCUS GOALS Fill in or check boxes as you complete.

THOUGHTS and scribbles.

WEEK-IN-REVIEW

Revisit your 3 focus goals and write down how you've done.

What were the highlights of the week? Victories? Defeats?

What did you learn about God this week?

What did you learn about yourself this week?

SHARE LIFE

TALK ABOUT

- Your conversations with God this week
- What you are learning and applying to your life from the Bible
- Whom you are investing in who doesn't know Jesus
- Any movement toward or away from your 3 focus goals

CONVERSATION NOTES:

What have you learned from each other?

How will you support and encourage each other this week? *Put a reminder on your calendar so you don't forget.*

NOTES or thoughts from the week.

Remain in Him. He'll take you where you need to go.

CHECK IN WITH YOURSELF

✳ LIFE CIRCLE | *5 minutes*

Use the Life Circle as a tool to ask yourself, "Do I feel satisfied or unsatisfied?" in each area. Fill in each slice accordingly.

✛ ASK YOURSELF WHY | *5 minutes*

Why are some slices fuller and others emptier? Talk to God and ask for wisdom.

🏆 SET FOCUS GOALS | *10 minutes*

Set 1 goal for 3 areas of the Life Circle you would like to focus on this week. Keep all goals specific and measurable, **then write down how you are going to prioritize it into your week.**

LIFE CIRCLE FOCUS AREA & GOAL	PRIORITIZE IT

☑ LIFE LIST | **OPTIONAL** | *10 minutes*

Do you need a comprehensive checklist to guide you through each category of the Life Circle?

It's called the Life List and it's FREE at **charityreeb.com**.

Consider using the Life List on weeks when you're feeling overwhelmed or need help making each area of the Life Circle actionable.

(Photo of the downloadable list maker)

BLOCK YOUR SCHEDULE | *10 minutes*

Your schedule reflects your priorities. Write in your 3 focus goals for this week, then build the rest of your schedule around them. Use a pencil so you can erase and rearrange.

	MORNING	AFTERNOON	NIGHT
M			
T			
W			
T			
F			
S			
S			

⚖️ BALANCE THE YESES AND NOES | *10 minutes*

Ask yourself, "What am I saying no to by saying yes to everything on this schedule? Will I regret that no?"

📦 UNPACK IT | *5 minutes*

Are you overcommitted? Intentionally lighten your load by either deferring something to next week or, when possible, asking someone for help.

Be
eternity-
minded

SPIRITUAL ESSENTIALS

READ anything from the Bible. Jot down what you read.

LEARN AND APPLY it to your real life. Jot down what you learned.

COMMIT concerns to God.

CONVERSE with God. Write a synopsis of your conversation.

MEDITATE on a word, theme, or verse found in scripture. Keep it true, pure, and positive.

JOURNALING

DEBRIEF the day.

A MOMENT you don't want to forget.

3 FOCUS GOALS Fill in or check boxes as you complete.

THOUGHTS and scribbles.

SPIRITUAL ESSENTIALS

READ anything from the Bible. Jot down what you read.

LEARN AND APPLY it to your real life. Jot down what you learned.

COMMIT concerns to God.

CONVERSE with God. Write a synopsis of your conversation.

MEDITATE on a word, theme, or verse found in scripture. Keep it true, pure, and positive.

JOURNALING

DEBRIEF the day.

A MOMENT you don't want to forget.

3 FOCUS GOALS Fill in or check boxes as you complete.

☐   ☐   ☐

THOUGHTS and scribbles.

SPIRITUAL ESSENTIALS

READ anything from the Bible. Jot down what you read.

LEARN AND APPLY it to your real life. Jot down what you learned.

COMMIT concerns to God.

CONVERSE with God. Write a synopsis of your conversation.

MEDITATE on a word, theme, or verse found in scripture. Keep it true, pure, and positive.

JOURNALING

3

DEBRIEF the day.

A MOMENT you don't want to forget.

3 FOCUS GOALS Fill in or check boxes as you complete.

THOUGHTS and scribbles.

4

SPIRITUAL ESSENTIALS

READ anything from the Bible. Jot down what you read.

LEARN AND APPLY it to your real life. Jot down what you learned.

COMMIT concerns to God.

CONVERSE with God. Write a synopsis of your conversation.

MEDITATE on a word, theme, or verse found in scripture. Keep it true, pure, and positive.

4

JOURNALING

DEBRIEF the day.

A MOMENT you don't want to forget.

3 FOCUS GOALS Fill in or check boxes as you complete.

THOUGHTS and scribbles.

SPIRITUAL ESSENTIALS

READ anything from the Bible. Jot down what you read.

LEARN AND APPLY it to your real life. Jot down what you learned.

COMMIT concerns to God.

CONVERSE with God. Write a synopsis of your conversation.

MEDITATE on a word, theme, or verse found in scripture. Keep it true, pure, and positive.

JOURNALING

DEBRIEF the day.

A MOMENT you don't want to forget.

3 FOCUS GOALS Fill in or check boxes as you complete.

THOUGHTS and scribbles.

SPIRITUAL ESSENTIALS

READ anything from the Bible. Jot down what you read.

LEARN AND APPLY it to your real life. Jot down what you learned.

COMMIT concerns to God.

CONVERSE with God. Write a synopsis of your conversation.

MEDITATE on a word, theme, or verse found in scripture. Keep it true, pure, and positive.

6

JOURNALING

DEBRIEF the day.

A MOMENT you don't want to forget.

3 FOCUS GOALS Fill in or check boxes as you complete.

THOUGHTS and scribbles.

WEEK-IN-REVIEW

Revisit your 3 focus goals and write down how you've done.

What were the highlights of the week? Victories? Defeats?

What did you learn about God this week?

What did you learn about yourself this week?

SHARE LIFE

TALK ABOUT

- Your conversations with God this week
- What you are learning and applying to your life from the Bible
- Whom you are investing in who doesn't know Jesus
- Any movement toward or away from your 3 focus goals

CONVERSATION NOTES:

What have you learned from each other?

How will you support and encourage each other this week? *Put a reminder on your calendar so you don't forget.*

NOTES or thoughts from the week.